KNOCK-KNOCK
JOKES
for
KIDS

Books by Rob Elliott

Laugh-Out-Loud Jokes for Kids
Laugh-Out-Loud Animal Jokes for Kids

KNOCK-KNOCK JOKES
for
KIDS

ROB ELLIOTT

SPIRE

© 2013 by Robert E. Teigen

Published by Revell
a division of Baker Publishing Group
P.O. Box 6287, Grand Rapids, MI 49516-6287
www.revellbooks.com

ISBN 978-0-8007-8822-3

Printed in the United States of America

The internet addresses, email addresses, and phone numbers in this book are accurate
at the time of publication. They are provided as a resource. Baker Publishing Group
does not endorse them or vouch for their content or permanence.

16   17   18   19   20   21   19   18   17

To "M," our foster son—
ever since you "knocked"
on the door of our hearts,
you have been a gift to our family.
You bring us laughter and love
every day that you're here.

Knock knock.
　　Who's there?
Amanda.
　　Amanda who?
Amanda fix the plumbing is here.

Knock knock.
　　Who's there?
Billy Bob Joe Penny.
　　Billy Bob Joe Penny who?
Seriously, how many Billy Bob Joe Penny's do you know?

Knock knock.
Who's there?
Weirdo.
Weirdo who?
Weirdo you think you're going?

Knock knock.
Who's there?
Leah.
Leah who?
Leah the door unlocked next time!

Knock knock.
Who's there?
Alden.
Alden who?
When you're Alden with your dinner, can you come out and play?

Knock knock.
Who's there?
Avery.
Avery who?
Avery nice person is knocking on the door. You should come take a look.

Knock knock.
Who's there?
Lena.
Lena who?
Lena little closer and I'll tell you another joke.

Knock knock.
Who's there?
Nick.
Nick who?
You're just in the Nick of time, I was getting ready to tell another knock-knock joke!

Knock knock.
　　Who's there?
West.
　　West who?
**Let me know if you need a west from these knock-
　　knock jokes.**

Knock knock.
　　Who's there?
Leon.
　　Leon who?
Leon me when you're not strong.

Knock knock.
　　Who's there?
Ash.
　　Ash who?
It sounds like you're catching a cold.

Knock knock.
  Who's there?
Mustache.
  Mustache who?
I mustache you a question, so let me in!

Knock knock.
  Who's there?
Jimmy.
  Jimmy who?
If you Jimmy a key I'll let myself in.

Knock knock.
  Who's there?
Will.
  Will who?
Will you listen to another knock-knock joke?

Knock knock.
Who's there?
Erin.
Erin who?
I have to run a quick Erin but I'll be back!

Knock knock.
Who's there?
Eddy.
Eddy who?
Eddy-body home?

Knock knock.
Who's there?
Oliver.
Oliver who?
Oliver doors are locked, let me in!

Knock knock.
   Who's there?
Alice.
   Alice who?
Well, you know what they say; Alice fair in love and
   war.

Knock knock.
   Who's there?
Wendy.
   Wendy who?
Wendy wind blows de cradle will rock.

Knock knock.
   Who's there?
Wayne.
   Wayne who?
Wayne drops are falling on my head, can you let me in?

Knock knock.
> Who's there?

Max.
> Max who?

Max no difference to me.

Knock knock.
> Who's there?

Toby.
> Toby who?

Toby or not Toby; that is the question, and you'll have to open up to find out!

Knock knock.
> Who's there?

France.
> France who?

France stick closer than a brother.

Knock knock.
    Who's there?
Peas.
    Peas who?
Peas tell me some more knock-knock jokes.

Knock knock.
    Who's there?
Gwen.
    Gwen who?
Gwen do you think you can come out and play?

Knock knock.
    Who's there?
Watson.
    Watson who?
Watson the radio?

Knock knock.
Who's there?
Wok.
Wok who?
I wok all the way here and you won't even let me come in!

Knock knock.
Who's there?
Yeast.
Yeast who?
You could at yeast come to the door and say hi!

Knock knock.
Who's there?
Collie.
Collie who?
Collie-flower is good for you.

Knock knock.
  Who's there?
Duncan.
  Duncan who?
Duncan cookies in milk is really yummy!

Knock knock.
  Who's there?
Sofa.
  Sofa who?
Sofa these have been good knock-knock jokes.

Knock knock.
  Who's there?
Window.
  Window who?
Window I get to hear some more knock-knock jokes?

Knock knock.
   Who's there?
Cheese.
   Cheese who?
For cheese a jolly good fellow, for cheese a jolly good fellow.

Knock knock.
   Who's there?
Boil.
   Boil who?
Boil you like this next joke!

Knock knock.
   Who's there?
Mushroom.
   Mushroom who?
There's mushroom for improvement on that last joke.

Knock knock.
    Who's there?
Pizza.
    Pizza who?
I'm going to give him a pizza my mind!

Knock knock.
    Who's there?
Pesto.
    Pesto who?
I hate to make a pesto myself, but I'm going to keep
    knocking until you open.

Knock knock.
    Who's there?
Gluten.
    Gluten who?
You're going to be a gluten for punishment if you don't
    open up!

Knock knock.
   Who's there?
Shellfish.
   Shellfish who?
Don't be shellfish, open up and share!

Knock knock.
   Who's there?
Darleen.
   Darleen who?
Please be a Darleen and open the door for me.

Knock knock.
   Who's there?
Les.
   Les who?
Les tell some more knock-knock jokes!

Knock knock.
  Who's there?
Gino.
  Gino who?
Gino, these knock-knock jokes are kind of fun.

Knock knock.
  Who's there?
Gladys.
  Gladys who?
I'm Gladys time for another knock-knock joke.

Knock knock.
  Who's there?
Otto.
  Otto who?
You really Otto open the door.

Knock knock.
  Who's there?
Earl.
  Earl who?
Earl to bed, Earl to rise.

Knock knock.
  Who's there?
Jewel.
  Jewel who?
Jewel have to let me in soon.

Knock knock.
  Who's there?
Hobbit.
  Hobbit who?
Sorry, telling knock-knock jokes is a bad hobbit I'm
  trying to break.

Knock knock.
Who's there?
Pasture.
Pasture who?
It's pasture bedtime, mister!

Knock knock.
Who's there?
Dee.
Dee who?
Dee cake is in Dee oven.

Knock knock.
Who's there?
Ben Hur.
Ben Hur who?
Ben Hur for a while now, can you let me in?

Knock knock.
Who's there?
Rupert.
Rupert who?
Rupert your left foot in, Rupert your left foot out.

Knock knock.
Who's there?
Radio.
Radio who?
Radio not, here I come!

Knock knock.
Who's there?
Allison.
Allison who?
Allison for someone to come to the door but I don't hear anybody coming.

Knock knock.
Who's there?
Sandy.
Sandy who?
Open up and let's go to the Sandy beaches.

Knock knock.
Who's there?
Penny.
Penny who?
Penny for your thoughts?

Knock knock.
Who's there?
Mickey.
Mickey who?
Mickey won't fit in the keyhole, can you let me in?

Emma: **Will you remember me in an hour?**
Anna: Yes.
Emma: **Will you remember me in a day?**
Anna: Yes.
Emma: **Will you remember me in a week?**
Anna: Yes.
Emma: **Will you remember me in a month?**
Anna: Yes.
Emma: **Will you remember me in a year?**
Anna: Yes.
Emma: **I don't think you will.**
Anna: Sure I will!
Emma: **Knock knock.**
Anna: Who's there?
Emma: **See, you forgot me already!**

Knock knock.
Who's there?
Yule.
Yule who?
Yule never know who it is unless you open the door!

Knock knock.
  Who's there?
Benjamin.
  Benjamin who?
I've Benjamin on my guitar all day!

Knock knock.
  Who's there?
Ear.
  Ear who?
Ear is another knock-knock joke—are
  you ready?

Knock knock.
  Who's there?
Waddle.
  Waddle who?
Waddle you do if I tell another knock-
  knock joke?

Knock knock.
　　Who's there?
Howl.
　　Howl who?
Howl I open the door if it's locked?

Knock knock.
　　Who's there?
Uno.
　　Uno who?
Uno who this is?

Knock knock.
　　Who's there?
Scott.
　　Scott who?
There's Scott to be a better knock-knock joke than this one!

Knock knock.
> Who's there?

Wanda.
> Wanda who?

Wanda come out and play?

Knock knock.
> Who's there?

Nobel.
> Nobel who?

There was Nobel so I had to knock!

Knock knock.
> Who's there?

Mabel.
> Mabel who?

Mabel isn't working right either.

Knock knock.
   Who's there?
Leaf.
   Leaf who?
I'm not going to leaf so you had better let me in!

Knock knock.
   Who's there?
Figs.
   Figs who?
Figs your doorbell, it's not working!

Knock knock.
   Who's there?
Butter.
   Butter who?
Butter open up—it looks like rain out here!

Knock knock.
    Who's there?
Udder.
    Udder who?
Would you like to hear an udder knock-knock joke?

Knock knock.
    Who's there?
Claws.
    Claws who?
Claws the window—it's cold in here!

Knock knock.
    Who's there?
Auntie.
    Auntie who?
Auntie going to let me in yet?

Knock knock.
Who's there?
Irish.
Irish who?
Irish you would open the door now!

Knock knock.
Who's there?
Rita.
Rita who?
Rita good book lately?

Knock knock.
Who's there?
Watson.
Watson who?
Can you tell me Watson your mind?

Knock knock.
  Who's there?
Annie.
  Annie who?
Annie thing you can do I can do better.

Knock knock.
  Who's there?
Annie.
  Annie who?
Annie chance you want to hear another
  knock-knock joke?

Knock knock.
  Who's there?
Myth.
  Myth who?
I myth seeing you!

Knock knock.
 Who's there?
Jacob.
 Jacob who?
Jacob your mind! Do you want to hear another knock-knock joke?

Knock knock.
 Who's there?
Stu.
 Stu who?
It's Stu late to ask any questions!

Knock knock.
 Who's there?
Justin.
 Justin who?
I think I got here Justin time!

Knock knock.
   Who's there?
Adolf.
   Adolf who?
Adolf ball hit me on the mouth and my lip swelled up.

Knock knock.
   Who's there?
Lionel.
   Lionel who?
Lionel always get you in trouble, so tell the truth!

Knock knock.
   Who's there?
Manny.
   Manny who?
How Manny knock-knock jokes do you want to hear?

Knock knock.
Who's there?
Dawn.
Dawn who?
Please Dawn leave me out here in the rain.

Knock knock.
Who's there?
Adore.
Adore who?
Adore is between you and me so please open up!

Knock knock.
Who's there?
Eamon.
Eamon who?
Eamon the mood for some more knock-knock jokes, how about you?

Knock knock.
    Who's there?
Quiche.
    Quiche who?
Can I have a hug and a quiche?

Knock knock.
    Who's there?
Countess.
    Countess who?
Does this countess a funny knock-knock joke?

Knock knock.
    Who's there?
Kenya.
    Kenya who?
Kenya open the door, please?

Knock knock.
  Who's there?
Shelby.
  Shelby who?
Shelby comin' around the mountain
  when she comes!

Knock knock.
  Who's there?
Owen.
  Owen who?
I'm Owen you some money, so open
  up and I'll pay you back.

Knock knock.
  Who's there?
Les.
  Les who?
Open the door and Les be friends!

Knock knock.
Who's there?
Norway.
Norway who?
**There is Norway I'm going to just stand
here, so open the door!**

Knock knock.
Who's there?
Nacho cheese.
Nacho cheese who?
That is nacho cheese, so give it back!

Knock knock.
Who's there?
You.
You who?
You-hoo, it's me, can I come in?

Knock knock.
 Who's there?
Betty.
 Betty who?
I Betty doesn't know who this is!

Knock knock.
 Who's there?
Robin.
 Robin who?
**No, Robin Hood. He steals from the rich and gives
  to the poor.**

Knock knock.
 Who's there?
Misty.
 Misty who?
I misty chance to see you—will you let me come in?

Knock knock.
Who's there?
Summer.
Summer who?
Summer these jokes are funny, but some aren't!

Knock knock.
Who's there?
Sharon.
Sharon who?
I'm Sharon my cookies if you'll let me in!

Knock knock.
Who's there?
Hayden.
Hayden who?
Come out and play Hayden go seek!

Knock knock.
   Who's there?
Asaid.
   Asaid who?
Asaid open the door, it's cold out here!

Knock knock.
   Who's there?
Sheri.
   Sheri who?
I'll Sheri my secret if you open the door!

Knock knock.
   Who's there?
Abby.
   Abby who?
Abby stung me on the leg—ouch!

Knock knock.
 Who's there?
Abel.
 Abel who?
Do you think you're Abel to let me in now?

Knock knock.
 Who's there?
Wallace.
 Wallace who?
Wallace fair in love and war!

Knock knock.
 Who's there?
Barry.
 Barry who?
It's Barry nice to meet you!

Knock knock.
  Who's there?
Isaac.
  Isaac who?
Isaac of knocking so please let me in!

Knock knock.
  Who's there?
Judith.
  Judith who?
Judith thought these knock-knock jokes would get
  old, but they don't!

Knock knock.
  Who's there?
Diane.
  Diane who?
I'm Diane to see you, so open the door!

Knock knock.
  Who's there?
Carrie.
  Carrie who?
Don't you Carrie that I'm out here knocking?

Knock knock.
  Who's there?
Taryn.
  Taryn who?
It's Taryn me up inside that you won't let me in!

Knock knock.
  Who's there?
Annette.
  Annette who?
Annette to use the bathroom, so please open the door!

Knock knock.
   Who's there?
Whale.
   Whale who?
Whale, whale, whale, I see your door
   is locked again!

Knock knock.
   Who's there?
Art.
   Art who?
Art-2 D-2. May the force be with you!

Knock knock.
   Who's there?
Dexter.
   Dexter who?
Dexter halls with boughs of holly!

Knock knock.
    Who's there?
B-C.
    B-C who?
I'll B-Cing you.

Knock knock.
    Who's there?
Hans.
    Hans who?
Hans up—you're under arrest!

Knock knock.
    Who's there?
Delores.
    Delores who?
Delores my shepherd, I shall not want.

Knock knock.
   Who's there?
Isabella.
   Isabella who?
Isabella the door not working?

Knock knock.
   Who's there?
Don.
   Don who?
Don you want to come out and play?

Knock knock.
   Who's there?
Woo.
   Woo who?
Don't get all excited. It's just a knock-knock joke!

Knock knock.
    Who's there?
Ketchup.
    Ketchup who?
Let me come in so we can ketchup.

Knock knock.
    Who's there?
Lego.
    Lego who?
Lego of the doorknob so I can come in!

Knock knock.
    Who's there?
Handsome.
    Handsome who?
Handsome food to me, I'm hungry!

Knock knock.
Who's there?
Wa.
Wa who?
What are you so excited about?

Knock knock.
Who's there?
Howie.
Howie who?
Do you know Howie doing?

Knock knock.
Who's there?
Train.
Train who?
Someone needs to train you how to open a door.

Knock knock.
   Who's there?
Cargo.
   Cargo who?
Cargo beep, beep and vroom, vroom!

Knock knock.
   Who's there?
Matt.
   Matt who?
**I'm standing on your welcome Matt but I don't feel
   very welcome right now.**

Knock knock.
   Who's there?
Nicole.
   Nicole who?
I'll give you a Nicole if you let me in.

Knock knock.
    Who's there?
Sherwood.
    Sherwood who?
Sherwood enjoy coming in and seeing you!

Knock knock.
    Who's there?
Ron.
    Ron who?
You can Ron but you can't hide!

Knock knock.
    Who's there?
Andy.
    Andy who?
He knocked Andy knocked but you won't let him in!

Knock knock.
   Who's there?
Stan.
   Stan who?
Stan back, I'm coming in!

Knock knock.
   Who's there?
Henrietta.
   Henrietta who?
Henrietta bug and now he has a stomachache.

Knock knock.
   Who's there?
Hummus.
   Hummus who?
Let me in and I'll hummus a tune.

Knock knock.
Who's there?
I am.
I am who?
Don't you even know who you are?

Knock knock.
Who's there?
Hike.
Hike who?
I didn't know you liked Japanese poetry. (Haiku)

Knock knock.
Who's there?
Pumpkin.
Pumpkin who?
A pumpkin fill up your flat tire.

Knock knock.
Who's there?
Darren.
Darren who?
I'm Darren you to tell a funnier knock-knock joke!

Knock knock.
Who's there?
Evie.
Evie who?
Evie wonder why I'm knocking at the door?

Knock knock.
Who's there?
Rufus.
Rufus who?
Call 911—the Rufus on fire!

Knock knock.
Who's there?
Wendy.
Wendy who?
Wendy last time you had your doorbell checked?

Knock knock.
Who's there?
Funnel.
Funnel who?
The funnel start once you let me in!

Knock knock.
Who's there?
Garden.
Garden who?
Stop garden the door and let me in!

Knock knock.
>Who's there?

I'm.
>I'm who?

Don't you know your own name?

Knock knock.
>Who's there?

Hammond.
>Hammond who?

Let's make some Hammond eggs for breakfast.

Knock knock.
>Who's there?

Butcher.
>Butcher who?

Butcher hand over your heart when you say the pledge of allegiance.

Knock knock.
Who's there?
Frank.
Frank who?
Can I be Frank and say I really want you to open the door?

Knock knock.
Who's there?
Peek-a.
Peek-a who?
Peek-a-boo!

Knock knock.
Who's there?
Passion.
Passion who?
I was just passion through and thought I would say hello.

Knock knock.
    Who's there?
Pasture.
    Pasture who?
It's way pasture bedtime so you'd better go to sleep!

Knock knock.
    Who's there?
Acid.
    Acid who?
Acid I would stop by, so here I am!

Knock knock.
    Who's there?
Elba.
    Elba who?
Elba happy to tell you another knock-knock joke!

Knock knock.
Who's there?
Kent.
Kent who?
I Kent see why you won't just open the door.

Knock knock.
Who's there?
Zany.
Zany who?
Zany body want to come out and play?

Knock knock.
Who's there?
Brandy.
Brandy who?
Cowboys Brandy cattle out on the ranch.

Knock knock.
>Who's there?

Dots.
>Dots who?

Dots for me to know and you to find out.

Knock knock.
>Who's there?

Frasier.
>Frasier who?

I'm a Frasier going to have to let me in eventually.

Knock knock.
>Who's there?

Woody.
>Woody who?

Woody like to hear another knock-knock joke?

Knock knock.
Who's there?
Little old lady.
Little old lady who?
Wow, I didn't know you could yodel!

Knock knock.
Who's there?
Freeze.
Freeze who?
Freeze a jolly good fellow, freeze a jolly good fellow.

Knock knock.
Who's there?
Roy.
Roy who?
Roy, Roy, Roy your boat gently down the stream.

Knock knock.
  Who's there?
Wallaby.
  Wallaby who?
Wallaby a monkey's uncle!

Knock knock.
  Who's there?
Ivan.
  Ivan who?
Ivan idea—let's tell more knock-knock jokes!

Knock knock.
  Who's there?
Vera.
  Vera who?
Is Vera way you could open the door?

Knock knock.
    Who's there?
Snow.
    Snow who?
Snow use—I'll never run out of knock-knock jokes!

Knock knock.
    Who's there?
Bond.
    Bond who?
You're bond to succeed if you try, try again.

Knock knock.
    Who's there?
Bruce.
    Bruce who?
I'll Bruce my knuckles if I keep on knocking!

Knock knock.
  Who's there?
Elsie.
  Elsie who?
Elsie you later!

Knock knock.
  Who's there?
Luca.
  Luca who?
Luca through the keyhole and you'll see who it is!

Knock knock.
  Who's there?
Waddle.
  Waddle who?
Waddle you give me if I stop knocking and go away?

Knock knock.
Who's there?
Wade.
Wade who?
Wade a minute—I want to tell you another knock-knock joke!

Knock knock.
Who's there?
Megan.
Megan who?
It's Megan me mad that you won't open the door!

Knock knock.
Who's there?
Ethan.
Ethan who?
Ethan if you don't open the door, I'll still like you.

Knock knock.
Who's there?
Ima.
Ima who?
Ima waiting to hear another knock-knock joke!

Knock knock.
Who's there?
Marilee.
Marilee who?
Marilee, Marilee, Marilee, Marilee, life is but a dream!

Knock knock.
Who's there?
Sorry.
Sorry who?
Sorry, I think I'm knocking on the wrong door.

Knock knock.
　　Who's there?
Aaron.
　　Aaron who?
The Aaron here is kind of stuffy.

Knock knock.
　　Who's there?
Ben.
　　Ben who?
Ben away for a while but I'm back now.

Knock knock.
　　Who's there?
Cantaloupe.
　　Cantaloupe who?
You cantaloupe—you're too young to get married!

Knock knock.
    Who's there?
Stan.
    Stan who?
I can't Stan it anymore, tell me another knock-knock
    joke.

Knock knock.
    Who's there?
Taylor.
    Taylor who?
Taylor another knock-knock joke!

Knock knock.
    Who's there?
Kay.
    Kay who?
Is it O-Kay if I tell another knock-knock joke?

Knock knock.
Who's there?
Ice cream soda.
Ice cream soda who?
Ice cream soda people can hear me!

Knock knock.
Who's there?
Yugo.
Yugo who?
Yugo first, and I'll go second.

Knock knock.
Who's there?
Vanessa.
Vanessa who?
Vanessa door going to open up?

Knock knock.
    Who's there?
Wilma.
    Wilma who?
Wilma breakfast be ready pretty soon?

Knock knock.
    Who's there?
Macon.
    Macon who?
I'm Macon my own key to open this door!

Knock knock.
    Who's there?
Rudy.
    Rudy who?
It's Rudy never says please or thank you.

Knock knock.
    Who's there?
Bonnie.
    Bonnie who?
My Bonnie lies over the ocean.

Knock knock.
    Who's there?
Theodore.
    Theodore who?
Theodore is locked so please let me in!

Knock knock.
    Who's there?
Anita.
    Anita who?
Anita hear another knock-knock joke!

Knock knock.
Who's there?
Olive.
Olive who?
Since Olive here, I think you should let me in!

Knock knock.
Who's there?
Sadie.
Sadie who?
If I Sadie magic word will you let me in . . . P-L-E-A-S-E?

Knock knock.
Who's there?
Michael.
Michael who?
I Michael you on the phone if you don't answer the door!

Knock knock.
Who's there?
Bill.
Bill who?
I'll pay the Bill for dinner if you open the door!

Knock knock.
Who's there?
Francis.
Francis who?
Francis in Europe and Brazil is in South America.

Knock knock.
Who's there?
Tokyo.
Tokyo who?
What Tokyo so long to open the door?

Knock knock.
    Who's there?
Olive.
    Olive who?
Olive you!

Knock knock.
    Who's there?
Hugo.
    Hugo who?
Hugo's first and I'll go second.

Knock knock.
    Who's there?
Colin.
    Colin who?
From now on I'm Colin you on the phone!

Knock knock.
Who's there?
Sarah.
Sarah who?
Sarah reason you're not opening the door?

Knock knock.
Who's there?
Donut.
Donut who?
Donut make you laugh when people tell knock-knock jokes?

Knock knock.
Who's there?
Mummy.
Mummy who?
Mummy said you can come out and play.

Knock knock.
Who's there?
Muffin.
Muffin who?
Muffin much going on around here.

Knock knock.
Who's there?
Coke.
Coke who?
Are you calling me crazy?

Knock knock.
Who's there?
Waffle.
Waffle who?
It's waffle that you still haven't opened the door!

Knock knock.
   Who's there?
Fannie.
   Fannie who?
If Fannie body calls, tell them I went
   to the store.

Knock knock.
   Who's there?
Kanga.
   Kanga who?
No, kangaroo.

Knock knock.
   Who's there?
Noah.
   Noah who?
Noah don't think I'll tell you another
   knock-knock joke!

Knock knock.
> Who's there?

Leaf.
> Leaf who?

Leaf me alone so I can read my joke book!

Knock knock.
> Who's there?

Della.
> Della who?

Open the door so I can Della 'nother knock-knock joke.

Knock knock.
> Who's there?

Reed.
> Reed who?

Reed a good book lately?

Knock knock.
Who's there?
Walt.
Walt who?
Walt! Who goes there?

Knock knock.
Who's there?
Philip.
Philip who?
Philip your water bottle if you're thirsty.

Knock knock.
Who's there?
Hawaii.
Hawaii who?
I'm doing fine, thanks. Hawaii doing?

Knock knock.
  Who's there?
Fanny.
  Fanny who?
Fanny you should ask!

Knock knock.
  Who's there?
Lorraine.
  Lorraine who?
Lorraine is coming down so give me an umbrella!

Knock knock.
  Who's there?
Randy.
  Randy who?
I Randy whole way here, so open up!

Knock knock.
　Who's there?
Reggie.
　Reggie who?
Reggie to open the door yet?

Knock knock.
　Who's there?
Rich.
　Rich who?
Rich knock-knock joke is your favorite?

Knock knock.
　Who's there?
Dwight.
　Dwight who?
Dwight key will get the door open.

Knock knock.
    Who's there?
Chad.
    Chad who?
Chad don't you recognize me? I'm your son!

Knock knock.
    Who's there?
Landon.
    Landon who?
Is it true cats always Landon their feet?

Knock knock.
    Who's there?
Les.
    Les who?
Les you think I'm a stranger, look through the keyhole
    and you will see.

Knock knock.
> Who's there?

Meg.
> Meg who?

Meg up your mind—are you going to let me in or aren't you?

Knock knock.
> Who's there?

Doris.
> Doris who?

If the Doris locked I can't come in.

Knock knock.
> Who's there?

New Hampshire.
> New Hampshire who?

New Hampshire you're not going to open the door.

Knock knock.
    Who's there?
Macon.
    Macon who?
You're Macon me mad with all this knocking I'm
    having to do!

Knock knock.
    Who's there?
Yukon.
    Yukon who?
It's okay, Yukon tell me!

Knock knock.
    Who's there?
Watson.
    Watson who?
Watson TV tonight?

Knock knock.
　　Who's there?
Pig.
　　Pig who?
**I'm going to pig the lock if you don't open the door
　　and let me in!**

Knock knock.
　　Who's there?
Juno.
　　Juno who?
Juno who this is, so open up already!

Knock knock.
　　Who's there?
Albert.
　　Albert who?
Do Alberts fly south for the winter?

Knock knock.
Who's there?
Alvin.
Alvin who?
We're Alvin a great time out here!

Knock knock.
Who's there?
Figs.
Figs who?
Figs your phone so I can give you a call!

Knock knock.
Who's there?
Alma.
Alma who?
Alma knock-knock jokes are really funny!

Knock knock.
    Who's there?
Alex.
    Alex who?
Alex the questions around here!

Knock knock.
    Who's there?
Sherwood.
    Sherwood who?
Sherwood be nice if you'd open the door.

Knock knock.
    Who's there?
Abbott.
    Abbott who?
Abbott time you asked!

Knock knock.
　Who's there?
Abel.
　Abel who?
Abel rings every time an angel gets its wings.

Knock knock.
　Who's there?
Annette.
　Annette who?
Annette another glass of water, open up!

Knock knock.
　Who's there?
To.
　To who?
To whom!

Knock knock.
  Who's there?
Pizza.
  Pizza who?
Pizza really nice guy.

Knock knock.
  Who's there?
Mickey.
  Mickey who?
**Mickey won't unlock this door, so please
  let me in!**

Knock knock.
  Who's there?
Cash.
  Cash who?
No thanks, I'd rather have some peanuts.

Knock knock.
>Who's there?

Luke.
>Luke who?

Luke through the window and you'll see who's knocking.

Knock knock.
>Who's there?

Roach.
>Roach who?

I roach you a letter but I wanted to deliver it in person.

Knock knock.
>Who's there?

Abby.
>Abby who?

Abby birthday to you, Abby birthday to you!

Knock knock.
    Who's there?
Alberta.
    Alberta who?
Alberta can't guess in a million years!

Knock knock.
    Who's there?
Anna.
    Anna who?
Anna one, Anna two, Anna three!

Knock knock.
    Who's there?
Dozen.
    Dozen who?
Dozen anyone ever open their door anymore?

Knock knock.
    Who's there?
Hair.
    Hair who?
Hair today and gone tomorrow.

Knock knock.
    Who's there?
Ken.
    Ken who?
Ken you hear me now?

Knock knock.
    Who's there?
Alpaca.
    Alpaca who?
Alpaca suitcase for our vacation.

Knock knock.
　　Who's there?
Dishes.
　　Dishes who?
Dishes me, open up!

Knock knock.
　　Who's there?
Candice.
　　Candice who?
Candice joke get any worse?

Knock knock.
　　Who's there?
Tibet.
　　Tibet who?
Early Tibet, early to rise.

Knock knock.
    Who's there?
Tank.
    Tank who?
You're welcome!

Knock knock.
    Who's there?
Andy.
    Andy who?
Andy shoots, Andy scores!

Knock knock.
    Who's there?
Owls.
    Owls who?
Why yes, they do!

Knock knock.
   Who's there?
Otter.
   Otter who?
You otter open the door and let me in!

Knock knock.
   Who's there?
Bacon.
   Bacon who?
I'm bacon some cookies. Do you want
   one?

Knock knock.
   Who's there?
Haven.
   Haven who?
Haven you heard enough of these knock-
   knock jokes?

Knock knock.
Who's there?
Anita.
Anita who?
Anita drink of water so please let me in!

Josh:Knock knock.
Leah:Who's there?
Josh:Banana.
Leah:Banana who?
Josh:Knock knock.
Leah:Who's there?
Josh:Banana.
Leah:Banana who?
Josh:Knock knock.
Leah:Who's there?
Josh:Banana.
Leah:Banana who?
Josh:Knock knock.
Leah:Who's there?
Josh:Orange.
Leah:Orange who?
Josh:Orange you glad this joke is over?

Knock knock.
   Who's there?
Pitcher.
   Pitcher who?
Bless you! Are you catching a cold?

Knock knock.
   Who's there?
Alex.
   Alex who?
Alex-plain when you open the door!

Knock knock.
   Who's there?
Elsie.
   Elsie who?
Elsie you later!

Knock knock.
  Who's there?
Ears.
  Ears who?
Ears looking at you, kid.

Knock knock.
  Who's there?
Lydia.
  Lydia who?
**The Lydia fell off and made a big mess out here; please
  open up.**

Knock knock.
  Who's there?
Nun.
  Nun who?
Nun of your business.

Knock knock.
    Who's there?
June.
    June who?
June know how long I've been knocking out here?

Knock knock.
    Who's there?
August.
    August who?
August of wind almost blew me away!

Knock knock.
    Who's there?
Spell.
    Spell who?
W-H-O.

Knock knock.
  Who's there?
Police.
  Police who?
Police come out and play with me!

Knock knock.
  Who's there?
Jamaica.
  Jamaica who?
Jamaica good sandwich? I'm hungry!

Knock knock.
  Who's there?
Ally.
  Ally who?
Ally really want to do is tell another knock-knock
  joke!

Knock knock.
    Who's there?
Eve.
    Eve who?
I'll Eve you alone if you want me to.

Knock knock.
    Who's there?
Whale.
    Whale who?
I'll start to whale if you don't let me in.

Knock knock.
    Who's there?
Ima.
    Ima who?
Ima really glad to see you today!

Knock knock.
Who's there?
Jonah.
Jonah who?
Jonah anybody who will open the door for me?

Knock knock.
Who's there?
Cain.
Cain who?
Cain you open the door for me, it's very cold out here!

Knock knock.
Who's there?
Dishes.
Dishes who?
Dishes a really dumb knock-knock joke!

Knock knock.
Who's there?
Ada.
Ada who?
Ada lot of sweets and now I feel sick!

Knock knock.
Who's there?
Adam.
Adam who?
Adam all up and see how much you have!

Knock knock.
Who's there?
Jell-o.
Jell-o who?
Jell-o, it's me again!

Knock knock.
> Who's there?

Barbie.
> Barbie who?

Barbie-Q.

Knock knock.
> Who's there?

Peas.
> Peas who?

Peas come outside and play with me!

Knock knock.
> Who's there?

Fanny.
> Fanny who?

**If Fanny body asks, tell them I'm not
home.**

Knock knock.
  Who's there?
Jess.
  Jess who?
Jess me and my shadow.

Knock knock.
  Who's there?
Queen.
  Queen who?
Queen as a whistle!

Knock knock.
  Who's there?
Baby oil.
  Baby oil who?
Baby oil will, and baby oil won't!

Knock knock.
    Who's there?
Canoe.
    Canoe who?
Canoe come out and play?

Knock knock.
    Who's there?
Oldest.
    Oldest who?
Oldest knocking is giving me a headache.

Knock knock.
    Who's there?
Woody.
    Woody who?
Woody like to hear another knock-knock joke?

Knock knock.
  Who's there?
Weed.
  Weed who?
Weed better go home—it's time for dinner!

Knock knock.
  Who's there?
Juan.
  Juan who?
I Juan to tell you another knock-knock joke.

Knock knock.
  Who's there?
Anita.
  Anita who?
Anita minute to think of another knock-knock joke.

Knock knock.
   Who's there?
Amos.
   Amos who?
Amos-quito bit me on the arm!

Knock knock.
   Who's there?
Andy.
   Andy who?
Andy bit me again.

Knock knock.
   Who's there?
Colin.
   Colin who?
I'll be Colin you later.

Knock knock.
 Who's there?
Rockefeller.
 Rockefeller who?
You can Rockefeller to sleep in his cradle.

Knock knock.
 Who's there?
Water.
 Water who?
Water your favorite knock-knock jokes?

Knock knock.
 Who's there?
Conner.
 Conner who?
**Conner tell me another joke that's as funny as the
 last one?**

Knock knock.
    Who's there?
Dragon.
    Dragon who?
Quit dragon your feet and open the door!

Knock knock.
    Who's there?
Ringo.
    Ringo who?
Ringo round the rosie!

Knock knock.
    Who's there?
Willie.
    Willie who?
Willie ever open the door and let me in?

Knock knock.
　Who's there?
Wanda.
　Wanda who?
I Wanda where I put my car keys.

Knock knock.
　Who's there?
Moe.
　Moe who?
Moe knock-knock jokes, please!

Knock knock.
　Who's there?
Ernest.
　Ernest who?
Ernest is full of eggs!

Knock knock.
    Who's there?
Taylor.
    Taylor who?
Taylor brother to pick up his toys.

Knock knock.
    Who's there?
Dewy.
    Dewy who?
Dewy have a key to open this door or do I have to go
    through the window?

Knock knock.
    Who's there?
Lettuce.
    Lettuce who?
Lettuce know when you can come out and play!

Knock knock.
   Who's there?
Radio.
   Radio who?
Radio not—here I come!

Knock knock.
   Who's there?
Nose.
   Nose who?
Nose anymore good knock-knock jokes?

Knock knock.
   Who's there?
Watt.
   Watt who?
Watt, you want to hear another knock-knock joke?

Knock knock.
    Who's there?
Juicy.
    Juicy who?
Juicy any monsters under my bed?

Knock knock.
    Who's there?
Alaska.
    Alaska who?
Alaska just one more time!

Knock knock.
    Who's there?
Yellow.
    Yellow who?
Yellow, how are you doing today?

Knock knock.
Who's there?
Raymond.
Raymond who?
Raymond me to buy milk at the store.

Knock knock.
Who's there?
Doughnut.
Doughnut who?
Doughnut open the door to strangers!

Knock knock.
Who's there?
Handsome.
Handsome who?
Handsome snacks over here—I'm really hungry!

Knock knock.
Who's there?
Rabbit.
Rabbit who?
Rabbit carefully—it's a special present!

Knock knock.
Who's there?
Sarah.
Sarah who?
Is Sarah doctor in the house?

Knock knock.
Who's there?
Oscar.
Oscar who?
Oscar silly question and get a silly answer!

Knock knock.
Who's there?
Who.
Who who?
What, are you an owl or something?

Knock knock.
Who's there?
Sombrero.
Sombrero who?
Sombrero over the rainbow.

Knock knock.
Who's there?
Gorilla.
Gorilla who?
Gorilla me a hamburger, I'm hungry!

Knock knock.
    Who's there?
Dwayne.
    Dwayne who?
Dwayne the bathtub—I'm dwowning!

Knock knock.
    Who's there?
Conrad.
    Conrad who?
Conrad-ulations! That was a great knock-knock joke!

Knock knock.
    Who's there?
Walter.
    Walter who?
Walter you doing here so early?

Knock knock.
    Who's there?
Everest.
    Everest who?
Everest, or is it work, work, work?

Knock knock.
    Who's there?
Lion.
    Lion who?
Quit lion around and open the door!

Knock knock.
    Who's there?
Zoo.
    Zoo who?
Zoo think you can come out and play?

Knock knock.
   Who's there?
Thatcher.
   Thatcher who?
Thatcher was a good knock-knock joke. Can you tell another one?

Knock knock.
   Who's there?
Peace.
   Peace who?
Peace porridge hot, peace porridge cold.

Rob Elliott has been a publishing professional for more than fifteen years and lives in West Michigan, where in his spare time he enjoys laughing out loud with his wife and four children.

Need More Laughs?

------------ ✳ ------------

Visit

LOLJokesForKids.com

to submit your own jokes,
receive FREE printable doodle pages,
and watch the video!

• • •

Laugh-Out-Loud Jokes for Kids

@loljokesforkids

Doodles for
Everyone!

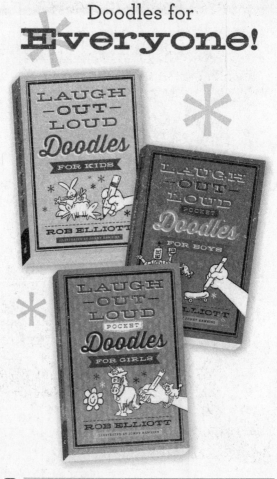

YOU AND YOUR KIDS HAVE A SPECIAL RELATIONSHIP.

Let Rob and Joanna Teigen show you how to make the most of it and build memories that will last a lifetime.

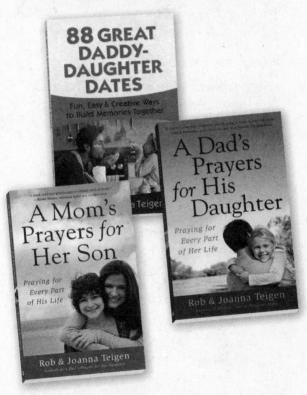